A Job at the Zoo

by Mike Craig

illustrated by Craig Smith

Harcourt Achieve

Rigby • Saxon • Steck-Vaughn

www.HarcourtAchieve.com
1.800.531.5015

Grandpa

Me

Man from
the zoo

Contents

Chapter 1

An Ad in the Paper

My grandpa really needed a job. One day he saw an ad in the paper. It was for a job at the zoo.

The ad didn't say what the job was.
But it did say the job was well paid.
Grandpa called the zoo. They asked
him to come in the next day.

"Have a seat," said the man from the
zoo. "As you may know, summer vacation
starts soon. It is our busiest time."

"The zoo needs lots of customers during the summer," the man said. "We have a lot of animals to feed. Without the money, the zoo will struggle."

"I see," Grandpa said.

"Our African gorilla is the animal everyone wants to see. He's our star attraction," the man said.

"But he's very ill. Without him the zoo will lose a lot of money."

Chapter 2

The Offer

"Hmm," Grandpa said, rubbing his chin.

The man from the zoo leaned forward.

He stared at Grandpa.
"Just how desperate are
you for work?"

"I'll do just about anything,"
Grandpa replied.

The man from the zoo smiled. "Good,"
he said, "because we want you to be
our gorilla."

12

"You want me to be a hairy ape?"
Grandpa shouted.

"Yes," replied the man, as if it was
nothing unusual. "We've flown in a
special suit from Hollywood."

"It's very realistic. No one will know the difference," the man from the zoo said, "and we'll pay you one thousand dollars a week."

"One thousand dollars!" Grandpa gasped. "That's a fortune. Show me the gorilla suit. I'll start right now!"

Chapter 3

The Show Begins

On the first day of vacation, thousands of children poured into the zoo. I went, too. Everyone rushed to see the gorilla.

Grandpa the gorilla was behind bars.
He was bounding around, jumping up on
rocks and over the grass.

The man from the zoo was right.
No one noticed that Grandpa was a
fake. Even I thought he looked real.

A thick rope hung from a tall tree.
Grandpa grabbed the rope and swung
from one side to the other.

Grandpa was putting on a show.

"Higher," I shouted.

So Grandpa swung higher.

"Higher," I shouted again.

So he swung higher still.

20

Suddenly he lost his grip on the rope.
He flew straight over the fence!

I gasped.

Chapter 4

The Growling Cave

Grandpa landed in a dirty pond. He stood up slowly. I was so glad that he wasn't hurt.

He waded to the edge of the pond.
Then he stopped.

A noise made Grandpa turn around.
A loud growl was coming out of a cave.

Grandpa froze in terror!

He'd landed in the lion's den!

A huge lion padded toward him.
Grandpa sank to his knees.

The lion crept nearer.

I couldn't look, so I closed my eyes. I waited for the lion's razor-sharp claws to tear into Grandpa's gorilla suit.

But the lion didn't strike.

Grandpa beat his chest loudly and ran into the cave. The show was over.

Later at home, Grandpa told me
what had happened. As the lion crept
toward him, Grandpa was so scared he
couldn't move.

Then the lion sniffed him and said,

"Don't worry, pal. We'll work something out — it's my first day here, too."

Glossary

customers
the people paying money for something

desperate
needy, ready to take any risk

fake
not real, false

Hollywood
the place where movies are made in California

padded
walked softly

realistic

looks like the real thing

star attraction

what everyone wants to see

struggle

trying hard to do something that is difficult

waded

walked through water

well paid

earned a lot of money

Mike Craig

When I was a boy, I saw a movie called *King Kong,* about a giant gorilla. I thought the creature was real, but my dad told me it was a man dressed in a monkey suit. "They do it all the time," said Dad. A few days later I went to the zoo. I made my way to where the gorillas lived. I checked them thoroughly, looking for any zippers . . .

Craig Smith